The CITADEL

of LEARNING

James Bryant Conant

BY THE SAME AUTHOR

On Understanding Science

Science and Common Sense

Education in a Divided World

Modern Science and Modern Man

Education and Liberty

The CITADEL
of LEARNING

New Haven:

Yale University Press

London:

Geoffrey Cumberlege:

Oxford University Press

1956

© 1956 by Yale University Press.
Printed in the United States of America by
Vail-Ballou Press, Binghamton, New York.
First published, March, 1956
Second printing, August, 1956
Library of Congress catalog card number: 56-5941

PREFACE

E V E R Y discussion of American schools and colleges must start from certain premises about the international situation. This has been true for at least a decade. In 1948 I stated my own assumptions in two introductory chapters in a book concerned with the public schools. The title of the volume, *Education in a Divided World,* summed up my forecast. I see no reason now to alter the prognosis I then made, namely that the world would remain divided for a long period of time but that the struggle between the two ideologies would not result in a global war. The three essays in the present volume are concerned with the work of scholars and teachers and not with international affairs. But my premise as to the future of world conditions is the starting point of all that follows. That a third world war would vitiate my reasoning and make irrelevant most of my conclusions is so obvious as hardly to require mention. Less obvious is the relation of the educational problems to the maintenance of freedom. Yet it is my belief that a successful solution of these problems is essential for the well being of the United States and therefore not without significance for the future of free men throughout the world. Whether I have argued my case well enough to convince others of the soundness of this conviction, the reader must decide.

The first chapter is based on the Spaulding Lecture delivered at Yale in February 1955; the second is an address delivered on the occasion of the celebration of the 100th anniversary of the founding of Michigan State College. I should like to record my appreciation of the invitation of these two universities which stimulated my thinking about American educational problems at a time when I was far distant from the scene.

Berlin, Germany,
September 25, 1955.

CONTENTS

1. *The Citadel of Learning,* 1

2. *An Old Tradition in a New World,* 23

3. *Some Basic Problems of American Education,* 49

The CITADEL

of LEARNING

1. THE CITADEL OF LEARNING

THE title of this essay might be: Reflections on the function of a university by a former college president while serving as United States High Commissioner in Berlin. My point of departure will be a consideration of the recent history of the famous University of Berlin.

When you pass through the Brandenburg Gate today, and enter the Russian Sector of Berlin, you soon come to the buildings of what was once Berlin University, now known as Humboldt University. During the Berlin blockade, when the Russian intent to sovietize the once-famous Berlin University became unmistakable, a group of students and professors left the old buildings, moved into temporary quarters in the American Sector of West Berlin and founded the now famous Free University of Berlin. This university, together with the Technical University (formerly the Technical High School) in the British Sector, carries

1

forward the great tradition of the German universities as it had developed before the Nazis seized control and did their best to poison these springs of learning. In the Russian Sector of Berlin and in the Russian Zone of Occupation, the universities passed from Nazi control to Soviet control—from one totalitarian regime to another. The way in which this transition was accomplished is an interesting story, for it illustrates how the Soviets in the first days of occupation threw a cloak of fine words about democracy over their true designs. They quickly replaced one authoritarian philosophy by another under the guise of serving the best interests of the German people. But this bit of history lies outside the scope of the present essay.

An organization of students in the Federal Republic, the German National Union of Students, published not long ago an interesting description of the sovietization of the universities in the Soviet Zone and Sector. On the flyleaf of this book is printed a quotation from Joseph Stalin which serves as leitmotiv for the account of what the Soviet occupying powers have attempted to accomplish. Freely translated, it reads as follows: "In front of us stands the citadel of learning. This citadel we must capture at any price. This citadel must be taken by our youth, if they wish to be the builders of a new life, if they wish, in fact, to take the place of the old guard."

2

The Citadel of Learning

Storm and capture the citadel of learning, so Stalin admonished Soviet youth some years ago. Concrete evidence of what such phrases mean can be obtained by visiting the University Bookstore in the Russian Sector of Berlin. Here one hunts in vain for copies of the works of the famous German philosophers, except for a slim volume of selections from Hegel's logic. But the shelves are full of volumes of the Marx-Lenin Library published in uniform bindings, primarily selections from the writings of Marx, Engels, Lenin, and Stalin. The demand for these books is a consequence of the requirement that all students in the university pass an examination in the course of Marxism-Leninism. The outline of this course and, particularly, the "required reading" illustrate what a strange dogmatic philosophy is now being dispensed to the students in the Soviet Zone and, I assume, throughout the Iron Curtain countries. Friedrich Engels' attack on the writings of one Herr Dühring and Lenin's long essay on *Materialism and Empiriocriticism,* first published in 1909, are two of the standard books, two books hardly regarded as worthy of attention by students of philosophy in the free nations of the world. Marxism-Leninism claims to be all-embracing; there is no field of learning where its proponents admit their doctrine is inapplicable; they have an answer to every question and an answer that allows no controversy, no rebuttal.

3

The Citadel of Learning

A recent number of one of the monthly publications in the Soviet Zone, *Einheit,* contains an article dealing with "The Philosophical Significance of the New Discoveries of the Soviet Astronomers." A discussion of such technical matters as the speed of expansion of the universe starts with the interesting statement that "the fight between materialism and idealism in the course of the development of science is particularly evident today in those fields of inquiry in which the results influence one's views of the universe." And in the course of the argument, it is stated as a self-evident proposition that "the philosophical point of departure for Soviet astronomy is dialectical materialism." Substitute in this sentence for the word "astronomy" the name of any field of intellectual endeavor, and you have summed up the regulations governing the activities of the inhabitants of the citadel of learning once this citadel has been stormed and captured. One and only one philosophical point of view is tolerated, namely that which goes under the name of dialectical materialism or Marxism-Leninism. "Education is concerned with truth, truth is everywhere the same, therefore education should be everywhere the same." This syllogism, attributed to an American educator, might well be inscribed over the doorway of every sovietized university. For no one uses the word "unity" more frequently than those who are attempting to force the

Soviet ideology on the people of the Russian Zone.

One of the propaganda devices used in taking over the universities in the Russian Zone was to insist that *all* education and *all* research have one and the same purpose and must be encompassed by one philosophy. This is one of the many false minor premises from which the Soviets start—that is, false if you accept the major premise of the necessity for free inquiry. The history of universities shows clearly that over the centuries they have had two distinct functions, which may be described as "the advancement of learning" and "advanced education." The first function transcends both time and space; it is largely independent of national boundaries and is continuous from generation to generation; the second, education, is determined by the social conditions of the community which the university serves at a particular period of history. It is with the first, the international function, the advancement of learning, that I am concerned when I use Stalin's phrase the "citadel of learning." It is this aspect of the life of a university that is illuminated by examining what has transpired among communities of scholars the other side of the Iron Curtain. For just as a study of pathological conditions in plants and animals may throw light on the conditions required for healthy growth, so, too, a study of Communist doctrine may be useful to us in an analysis of the role of our scholarly institutions in the free world. By realizing what happens when the citadel of learning has been captured, we may be better able to understand what is the essence of the activities within this citadel when it remains free.

Within the citadel of learning are to be found, according to my way of thinking, all those creative activities of the human spirit which are not directly related to practical affairs. Admittedly, a consideration of these activities takes one outside of a university. Men and women studying, thinking, and writing in libraries, research institutes, museums, and universities, as well as the lone scholar, writer, and artist—all have one attribute in common: *They are all engaged in a creative activity whose product each one hopes will have significance for a long period of time.* To the degree that a scientist or scholar is dedicated to the advancement of learning as such, his ambition must be to contribute to a long-range human enterprise, not to an immediate undertaking. Indeed, the ambition of all those to whom I am referring is summed up in the famous words of John Milton, when he wrote of his desire "to leave something so written to aftertimes, as they should not willingly let it die."

I have heard it said that there are areas of science and scholarship which are essentially neutral in the conflict between the Soviet ideology and that of the free world. I think an examination of what is going on in the Russian Zone of Occupation would prove that such a statement is not correct. It would be more accurate to say that while the Soviet system attempts to put its stamp on every activity, there are areas of scientific knowledge which have proved relatively resistant. To be sure, the philosophic implications of the theories of physics and chemistry must be in accord with the premises of dialectical materialism, but the so-called facts of these sciences are usually presented in much the same way in the textbooks used on both sides of the Iron Curtain. Biology, on the other hand, as the recent discussion of the Lysenko doctrine made evident, is a field where the imprint of the official philosophy is clearly to be seen. And every phase of the study of man's past or his behavior must bear the seal of the official dogma. In these areas of inquiry, it is difficult to find any agreement between the writers of the Western world and those under Soviet control. If anyone in the free world believes that a unifying philosophy is a goal to be desired at whatever price, then he should drive from the free sectors of Berlin eastward through the Brandenburg Gate.

Freedom and tolerance go hand in hand in matters of the spirit. The premises of an argument cannot be truly examined unless alternative premises are believed and defended by one or more persons of integrity and

scholarly competence. It is the absence of dissenters
from the official dogma that signalizes the capture of
the citadel of learning. Conversely, it is the presence
of defenders of different sets of premises that has in
the past ensured the vigorous development of the
Western tradition that stems from the ancient Greeks.
Not that the development has been continuous over
the last two thousand years. But in those lands and at
those times when there has been a flowering of intellectual and artistic activity, there has likewise been
violent dissension among scholars and artists—a dissension often resulting in bitter recriminations and
vindictive personal feuds.

These quarrels among scholars of other days, be they
theologians, humanists, scientists, or artists, are often
passed by hurriedly by historians, particularly the historians of the advancement of learning. For as judged
by the enthusiastic portrayer of the growth of cumulative knowledge, the quarrels are regrettable incidents,
the exceptional cases where certain scientists wandered
off the true path of progress; the less said about hy-
potheses now obsolete the better, particularly if the
proponents and opponents showed bad temper in their
debates! It is true that if one sets out to write a history
of the advancement of learning as a history of secular
saints, then the polemics between scholars and scientists
had best be left to footnotes, for the unlovely aspects

of human nature are apt to be quite manifest in such writings.

According to my view, instead of passing by the disputes of learned men, we would do well to put them in the foreground of our description of the intellectual and artistic activities of previous generations. For it is as a very human adventure of quarrelsome individuals that the advancement of learning must be seen to be understood. Eliminate the quarrels from the story of the past, and it all seems only a matter of time and patient labor before the storehouse of cumulative knowledge will be as full as anyone may desire. Eliminate the quarrelers, as is done in the captured citadel, and you get only further accumulation of knowledge in terms of the premises frozen into the philosophy of the state. (I may remark parenthetically that in the Soviet countries today this set of conditions does, of course, allow progress to be made in the physical sciences, temporarily at least. No one would want to minimize the capacity of the Soviet Union to proceed with speed and effectiveness in technological affairs.)

Controversy is essential to a healthy condition in the citadel of learning. But such a statement is not a definition. One may well ask, what is the essence of the undertaking on which so much creative effort has been expended, so many quarrels engendered over tens of centuries? Is it not an attempt—a continued and never-ending attempt—to find what fancies of the human brain are warranted and what are not? So it seems to me. To test beliefs by various methods, to find standards by which interpretations of tragedy and joy may be evaluated, to find standards for assessing common-sense judgments of good and evil, for accepting new ideas as part of the cultural heritage or rejecting them as passing illusions of a disordered brain—such are the tasks of the dwellers in the citadel of learning.

Perhaps some of you may be inclined to say, why not sum it all up by the ancient phrase "the search for the truth"? Since "Veritas" is on the Harvard shield, this is a particularly attractive gambit for a former Harvard administrative officer, and I admit to having employed it in my youth. But that there are grave and complex difficulties in answering Pontius Pilate's question What is truth? all who are conversant with the history of the theory of knowledge will readily agree. Nor are the difficulties entirely of a technical philosophic nature. William James discovered to his sorrow how easy it was for a popular account of an epistemological theory to be misunderstood once the apparently simple word "truth" was placed in the forefront of the discussion.

There is a complaint current among laymen today that the philosophers have turned mathematicians— that is, in the free world, of course; on the other side of the Iron Curtain they are expounders of a dogma. It is true that some of the most brilliant of the younger philosophers are concerned with the type of problems to which Whitehead and Russell devoted their attention in their famous work *Principia Mathematica*. But this seems to me no cause for lamentation. For surely the question of the warrant for our belief in the theorems of mathematics is as fundamental a problem as one can well imagine. After all, why are all of us willing to stake our lives on the correctness of the proposition that $2 \times 2 = 4$? What is the warrant for this belief? In spite of many centuries of an enormous expenditure of energy, there is no agreed-on answer to this basic question, the nature of mathematical truth. Nevertheless, highly significant discoveries in mathematics and logic have been made in the course of the exploration, particularly during the last hundred years. A body of knowledge has been generated that "aftertimes . . . will not willingly let die." Some of it may later be found to contain unwarranted assumptions or deductions built into the framework, but such later findings, if they occur, will not invalidate the significance of the entire undertaking viewed as a creation of man's spirit.

Professor Quine has recently written as follows (and I hope I am not quoting him out of context): "The totality of our so-called knowledge or beliefs, from the most casual matters of geography and history to the profoundest laws of atomic physics or even of pure mathematics and logic, is a man-made fabric which impinges on experience only along the edges." If I may be permitted to continue Professor Quine's metaphor without holding him responsible for what follows, I would say that the physical sciences are involved only along one edge of this fabric of many edges. Along this one particular edge, experimental investigations proceed from time to time to produce results that require readjustments within the fabric. The so-called positive nature of science is due to the unanimity among experts as to the nature of the readjustments required to accommodate new experimental results.

Along other edges of the man-made fabric of ideas, philosophers have been quarreling for many centuries. Here there has been relatively little unanimity of opinion. Not only have there been rival metaphysical systems, but conflicting views as to the formulation of principles of ethics, of politics and, in recent centuries, of economics. Historians and archaeologists have likewise had, and still have, their disputed areas; philologists as well. Few would be inclined to quarrel with the summation of all these activities as a search for warranted beliefs. But some readers may well object to my designating scientific knowledge as warranted belief. For there are those who maintain that a scientific hypothesis such as the atomic theory may be proved correct or incorrect by essentially the same procedures as are used in everyday life in testing the validity of minor hypothetical statements. For example, it is claimed that experiments have established our modern views as to the structure of matter, in the same sense of the word *establish* as used in the sentence, "I can readily establish by returning to the hall the correctness or incorrectness of my belief that I failed to put out the front hall light when I came upstairs a few moments ago."

My own interpretation of the nature of physical science is more in accord with the statement I have quoted from Professor Quine. The present scientific conceptual scheme is a total fabric. We cannot take one portion of it and state that its validity is established by a set of experiments. We can see clearly in retrospect how at various stages in the development of physics and chemistry in the last four hundred years alternative concepts could be employed for a time with equal satisfaction. Considerations of convenience, simplicity, and elegance to some degree dictated the finally accepted choice. Indeed, today, we might devise substitutes for portions of our theoretical framework if we were willing to throw these same considerations to the winds.

Furthermore, it seems clear that the development of our modern scientific ideas might have taken a somewhat different course, if the chronological se-

13

quence of certain experimental findings had been different. And to some degree, at least, this chronology can be regarded as purely accidental. In this connection, a consideration of the history of the atomic theory since 1800 is of value. A book could be written on the ups and downs of the chemist's belief in the reality of atoms. In the second quarter of the nineteenth century the theory was on the point of being abandoned. Then again toward the close of the century some important philosophers of science predicted that the theory would soon disappear since it was a naïve attempt to depict the structure of matter; chemistry could be better formulated in terms of energy relations. A short-lived and very inaccurate prediction, we now say. Yet if the scientists of the 1880's and 1890's were to come to life today, they might make a case that the atomic theory *which they knew* had been abandoned and replaced by a new one. For what sort of elementary particles are these, they would ask, which have centers but no boundaries? And what sort of nonsense is this to speak of the fission of the atom of an element since an atom by definition is indivisible and an element a substance not subject to decomposition! Our reply is obvious; we have had to remake the old atomic theory to accommodate new experimental data. And, we might add, if the concepts of *your* theory had not become so imbedded in the fabric of our chemical knowledge, we might have thrown your terminology overboard and thus avoided some present difficulties in definition of atoms, elements, and atomic weights. Which would amount to saying, tradition as well as convenience plays a role in shaping our scientific thoughts.

In reviewing the history of science we encounter, of course, some former beliefs now unwarranted which nevertheless continue to be current because of their convenience. These scientific fictions—or myths, to use the theological term—are significant for pedagogy and within limited areas for practical purposes as well. Thus engineers often speak of the flow of heat as though heat were an imponderable fluid, and use the concept in calculations. The principles of navigation are most readily taught with the aid of a model in which the sun and stars revolve about the earth. The first introduction to the physics of mirrors and lenses can hardly be accomplished without explicitly or implicitly bringing in a medium in which light may be supposed to travel as waves.

The question of the warrant for a belief has thus been repeatedly raised in the history of science. But the controversies which have raged about the validity of scientific theories have been remarkably short-lived *since the sixteenth century*. As a consequence, there have been relatively few cases where emotional bias and personal feuds have intruded themselves for more than a few years in the teaching of science. As I read the record, this has been in part a consequence of the vast number of laboratory workers who were daily employing the conceptual fabric. Alternative theories with alternative terminologies spell confusion; one had to get ahead with the advancing science by agreeing on convenient and relatively simple modifications of the older concepts. Occasionally this process has required a decade or two. Those who remember the battles about the introduction of the ionic theory will recall hearing certain older professors of chemistry declare they certainly did not *believe* in these new notions about ions.

What are the warrants for belief in the ionic theory, in the validity of the present methods for determining the age of the universe, in the present dating of the Mycenaean age? These questions are surely essentially of the same character. So, too, it seems to me, are the following questions: What is the warrant for the belief that a certain city will benefit by adopting the city manager system? What is the warrant for the belief that the old mercantile theory of evaluating trade is incorrect? What are the warrants for belief that the prosperity of the United States in the first half of the twentieth century was due to the tariff policy? Admittedly the warrants for beliefs about systems of government or validity of economic analyses or policies are very different from the warrants appealed to by chemists, geologists, astronomers, archaeologists, or historians. But would not the professors of all the many disciplines represented in a modern university respond each with the same degree of indignation if he or she were accused of a *professional* belief that was *un*-warranted?

But just a moment, you may say, what about the professors of the philosophy of religion and the theologians? Is it not inherent in the nature of religious belief that it is unwarranted? The affirmative answer to this question has been itself the subject of much controversy. Whatever side the reader may care to take in this discussion, it is quite clear that rival religious ideas have had and still have a special impact on the emotional attitudes of men and women of the Western world. Nonetheless scholars have piled argument on argument as warrants for their beliefs. Unlike the conceptual schemes of the sciences, the beliefs in question are not an extension of the common-sense ideas which enabled primitive man to manipulate inanimate nature. We are not dealing here with a gradual expansion of a mass of interconnected concepts which have proved themselves to be sure guides to practical manipulations. In short, we are not dealing with cumulative theoretical knowledge. Therefore, the search for warranted beliefs

17

along this edge of experience has usually led to the formation of coherent groups of scholars standing in opposition to one another, each defending warranted belief (orthodoxy) and attacking error (heresy).

The basic experiences that are here involved are not related to man's practical achievements in shaping tools, controlling fire, growing crops, organizing governments, or promoting trade and manufacture. They are far more personal experiences, yet experiences almost without exception involving other human beings. A man's joys, sorrows, above all his loves and hates, are the basic data to which are added statements by contemporaries, and those left by earlier men and women about their own experiences.

What religious beliefs are warranted from a study of written documents? What beliefs are warranted as to the future of an individual, of a nation, of the human race? These questions, unlike the question of the reality of neutrinos, touch the life of even the most unsophisticated men and women. They can be partially brushed aside, to be sure, during holiday moods, but in those times when catastrophe and tragedy are everywhere apparent, they become for many *the* important questions. Even in relatively quiet times the answers often arouse strong loyalties and violent emotions. And at periods in the past, differences in beliefs have been the slogans for men who have devastated nations. But such wars and persecutions are not a necessary consequence of the quarrels of theologians; they are rather manifestations of man's desire for power and his fear of hostile groups. Therefore, in spite of the historical record left by their partisan supporters, all theologians who as scholars have been engaged in the quest for *warranted* beliefs must be honored as dwellers in the citadel of learning.

And the poet and the artist, are they, too, to be counted as working within the walls of the same citadel? Yes, according to my view, though I shall not attempt to maintain that they are engaged in a quest for warranted beliefs. I do suggest, however, that they are concerned with a closely related and equally controversial undertaking—a search for a warranted interpretation of man's emotional experiences. I have already interpreted the usual pattern of the pursuit of certainty, namely mathematics and science, in such a way that this search differs in degree but not in kind from the studies of theologians and metaphysicians. And to say that philosophy and poetry often merge is to utter a commonplace. Indeed, the edge of experience with which the poet or artist is concerned overlaps in large part that of the metaphysician, but the emotional content is here of prime importance. And the warrants—what are they? Some would maintain, only the artist's own feelings. If that were true, then such a completely individualistic affair would indeed fall outside the bounds of what we are concerned with here. Even in the heart of the Soviet Union I suppose a poet may safely scribble any poem he may desire, provided he immediately destroys the evidence of his independence as a creative artist. But few writers and few painters have failed to share with Milton an "inward prompting" that they might perhaps leave something that aftertimes "should not willingly let die." The interpretations of the poet or artist are thus warranted to a greater or lesser degree by the judgment of future generations.

Scholars tend to find the warrants for their beliefs by examining the records of the past; the poet and artist, like the scientist, must look to the future for his justification. "So beautiful, so significant, that it was not only full of meaning for many contemporaries but has been admired by subsequent generations"—if this can be said about a poem, a picture, a building, surely one is warranted in saying, here is a warranted interpretation of the significance of man's spiritual existence!

I shall push no further this attempt to find the common basis for the work of poets, philosophers, and scholars. Some will certainly reject the premises of my argument, particularly as regards science and mathematics. But whatever philosophic orientation determines the reader's evaluation of the work of scientists and scholars, he will hardly disagree that what is at issue is no trivial affair. From whatever angle our art, literature, philosophy, and science are viewed, there can be no doubt that they have been the product of both conflict and cooperation, both a struggle among beliefs and a sharing of beliefs. These are the terms on which those within the citadel of learning have lived and worked effectively in the past; these are the only terms which will ensure the safety and vitality of this citadel in the future. Yet these terms are denied and ridiculed today by the rulers of vast and powerful nations. Therefore, it seems important that we should not minimize what is at issue in the challenge. It seems important that we should not minimize the vastness of this man-made fabric—the richness of the golden cloth of learning.

Whether, in terms moral and political, recorded history warrants a belief in the doctrine of progress may be an open question. But, however negative one's views may be as to the general applicability of this notion, it certainly is applicable to large areas of past intellectual activity. Perhaps many of the works of art still carefully preserved from former times might well have perished, perhaps whole libraries of the works of certain theologians, philosophers, and scholars are completely without warrant: still, taking the labors as a whole, one must admit to the grandeur of the undertaking. As a member of the human race, one must contemplate with pride the labors of those who have worked and argued to advance learning through the centuries. And today with the world divided, scholars and laymen in all the free nations need to reaffirm their resolution to see to it, as far as lies within their power, that the international flag of freedom continues to fly above an inviolate citadel of learning.

2. AN OLD TRADITION

IN A NEW WORLD

T H E establishment of land-grant colleges nearly a hundred years ago was one of two contemporary revolutionary steps which transformed the idea of a university in the United States; the other was the development of the four-year college. The Morrill Act of 1862 granting federal land to each of the states to support "such branches of learning as are related to agriculture and the mechanic arts" was an expression of the new outlook on education. Agricultural colleges had been established in several states in the mid-fifties, and there was a growing recognition of the need for institutions "to promote the liberal and practical education of the industrial classes in the several pursuits and professions in life." For the middle of the last century was a period when the spreading of knowledge, particularly practical knowledge, to all the inhabitants of the United States became a dominant idea.

Public libraries were opened; mechanic arts institutes were being founded. What was happening involved more than the transformation of the idea of a university; it involved the development of a totally new educational tradition. European ideas about schools and universities were in less than a century to be re-shaped into a characteristic American educational tradition.

With these thoughts in mind, I have chosen for the title of this essay "An Old Tradition in a New World" —the new world being, of course, America; the old tradition, the European tradition of education. But the title has a double meaning; for I intend to raise some questions about the impact of the constricted yet divided world of nuclear weapons in which we now live —the impact of *this* new world on what is now, at least in the United States, an old tradition, namely the American concept of education.

Every American citizen is proud of what our publicly supported universities and colleges have done and are now doing to promote the welfare of the United States. And whether it be general education, or specialized education or research (pure and applied), we find land-grant institutions in the forefront. Therefore it is quite unnecessary to recount the triumphs of these characteristically American institutions. But it is perhaps of some value to consider American education as a whole; in particular, to spell out the essential differences between the European educational tradition and the American. A failure to appreciate the nature of these differences is evident in the writings of the few proponents of the older tradition who are still vocal in the United States. These people, some of whom were themselves educated in Europe, fail to realize the nature of the mutation that education has undergone in the last century in America. Therefore, their criticism of our schools and colleges is often not only harsh but unrealistic, and consequently not constructive.

Like everything else on the continent of Europe, education is not what it was a century ago. Nevertheless, I think it would be fair to say that in comparison to the revolutionary changes on the American continent the European educational tradition has remained essentially unaltered. I speak, of course, only of education in the free European countries; what has happened the other side of the Iron Curtain is another story which was in part recounted in my discussion of the sovietization of the schools and universities in the Russian Zone of Occupation in Germany. In what follows I shall confine my comparison to education in the free nations of Europe on the one hand and in the United States on the other. And in so doing I want to make it abundantly clear at the outset that I am not passing a judgment on the absolute merits of the

25

two systems: I am not recommending that any European country take over the American concept of education, and I am most assuredly not advocating that we revert to the European.

The reasons for the conservatism of Europe on educational matters, on the one hand, and for the revolutionary nature of the American developments, on the other, are to be found in the social history of the two continents. One of the basic differences between Europe and the United States in the last hundred years can be described by the word mobility. Here on the North American continent we have had a high degree of both geographic and social mobility; in Western Europe a relatively low degree. In European countries, before World War II, the vast majority of people in all walks of life grew up and died in the community in which they and their grandparents were born. In living the life of established local customs, these men and women were not bowing before hard necessity but gladly and freely leading the sort of existence that seemed honorable and good. Wars, famine, and natural catastrophes may require people to move, but the normal way of life, the desired way of life, is to stay where you were born—so argued the Europeans.

In the United States in the nineteenth century the push toward the West and the flood of immigrants from overseas forced our society into a state of movement. The advent of the automobile has tended to perpetuate this condition. As seen from the other side of the Atlantic Ocean, we are still a restless folk, without roots or local customs. Furthermore, we are by comparison still a fluid society with a relative absence of hierarchies and class barriers. And this fact is again explicable in terms of our history. Closely related to the impulse to move from town to town, or state to state, was the desire to better one's lot economically and socially. And for vast numbers of Americans this impulse coincided with opportunity. I realize that it can be argued that in the last fifty years both the desire for and the opportunity to attain a higher social status have been less than in the second half of the nineteenth century. That may be so; but at the same time many things which in the past largely determined social status have been vastly altered. Because of changing financial rewards, there has developed to an amazing degree in many parts of the United States a type of society in which the sociologist is hard put to it to discover a dominant social hierarchy. Certainly a servant class in the European sense has vanished. European visitors are surprised at the variety of occupations in which a person can be engaged without affecting the way he is regarded by the community.

This mixed-up, confused society of ours is something which I believe most Americans, when they view it objectively, view with pride—just as they take pride in the fact that America has been and still is the land of opportunity. Indeed, when I attempt to sum up for Europeans American education in terms of American idealism, I say the development of our schools and colleges has been motivated by our desire to move constantly toward two goals: equality of opportunity for all youth, equality of respect for all honest citizens.

Was it not this doctrine of equality of respect that was taken over by the academic profession in the United States a century ago when agricultural and mechanical arts colleges were founded and sustained? Has not the whole American educational tradition been the development of a tradition in which the equality of all useful labor was recognized? So it seems to me. Implicit or explicit, these twin ideals—equality of opportunity and equality of respect—as goals have guided the work of countless teachers in the United States.

The universities of Europe underwent but little change during the last hundred years. They are today as they were in the second half of the nineteenth century, institutions attended by young people for the purpose of preparing themselves for a few traditional professions. These young people have considerable academic ability and have had long years of rigorous school training. In the university the emphasis is as far as possible on the theoretical and the abstract, the general as contrasted to the particular. The contrast between education as exemplified in a university and training in a trade school is underlined.

To be sure, engineers and economists as well as doctors, lawyers, theologians, and future teachers and professors are educated in the schools of higher learning in Europe. But the nature of the instruction, the limitation of the concept of a profession, and above all the selection of the students make European universities almost as different from American as fall is from spring. A student to be admitted to a university must have completed a special course that begins usually at age eleven or twelve and runs about six years. I use the words "special course" in two senses: by American standards it is a specialized course because of its emphasis on acquiring such intellectual skills as the command of one or two foreign languages; special also in the sense that almost without exception such courses of instruction are given in separate schools. Though I might mention an interesting experiment in one German town near Darmstadt; the special university preparatory school in this exceptional instance is part of a school community serving all the children of the neighborhood.

The separation of those who are preparing to enter a university thus occurs early by American standards

29

and is socially as well as educationally a complete separation; furthermore, the numbers involved are, by our standards, few. Not more than 10 per cent of an age group are enrolled in university preparatory schools in any European country. Since those who are not chosen for these special schools complete their schooling at age fourteen or fifteen, we find less than 10 per cent of the sixteen-year-olders enrolled in full-time education in Europe; the corresponding figure in the United States is 75 per cent. And while I am giving statistics, I might point out that the European universities enroll less than 5 per cent of those who are of the age to attend, while in the United States we enroll in colleges and universities (on a full-time basis) something like 30 per cent. In short, our methods of educating youth in the United States differ from those in Europe as to the percentage of the age group enrolled, as to the age at which the university preparatory course begins, and as to social separation of the pupils headed for higher education.

An American is, naturally, curious as to how, under the European scheme, the relatively few are selected who start to prepare for a university at an early age. He is not likely to obtain a clear and simple answer to his question. In the nineteenth century, the university students in Europe largely came from families with an inherited position or recently acquired wealth. Family income and social position still play a role today but are by no means the predominant factors. The situation varies not only from nation to nation but from community to community within a nation. By and large one can say that there is a widespread belief in Europe, as there is in America, in the importance of finding talent and developing it, irrespective of family status. But the difficulties of reconciling this objective with the traditional educational practice are considerable. How is one to decide at age eleven or twelve which are in fact the most promising children?

The British experience since the end of World War II in this matter of selecting students for different schools is most illuminating. Attempts to make the selections purely on the basis of demonstrated capacity for schoolwork as tested by examinations have evoked widespread public criticism. The problem appears to be far from solved and the current discussion underscores the consequences of trying to maintain the European concept of a university in a period when individual freedom and equality of opportunity are dominant ideals. The flexible arrangement of schools and colleges in the United States enables us to avoid one set of difficulties. We do not try to make a rigorous selection at age eleven or twelve: we offer a variety of choices over a period of years, and many a youth does not decide until sixteen or seventeen whether to

31

go to college or not. Furthermore, the relatively large percentage of our youth who attend a college or university, the great variety of subjects that can be studied in these institutions, and the wide range of standards blur the sharp distinctions between one kind of education and another which are inherent in the European pattern.

Of course, the European university system must be considered in relation to the European apprentice system; these are two complementary parts of the same picture. In Europe, the boy who has not been enrolled in a university preparatory course will usually be found working as an apprentice at age fifteen; his further schooling will be one day a week or in the evenings. Our young people enter into industrial work at a later age and by a variety of routes. It has become the accepted thing for American youth, all our youth, to be in school, full-time, at least until they are seventeen or eighteen years of age. This, which sounds obvious common sense to us, is in fact a recent American invention.

The American tradition was formed by the circumstances of this nation during the second half of the nineteenth century. The land-grant college movement with its emphasis on the importance of higher education as a preparation for practical life was one of two manifestations of a peculiarly American point of view. The other was the persistence of that unique American institution, the four-year college. Both affected the schools throughout the nation by underlining the importance of full-time education at a degree-granting institution. But the land-grant college movement, by widening enormously the range of professional university work, had perhaps the greater impact on the curriculum of the secondary schools. If, as in Europe, study in a university is confined to a relatively few professions, it becomes possible to define the nature of a university preparatory course. But when the scope of university work has been expanded as it has in the United States the whole idea of a college preparatory course loses its meaning. It becomes impossible and undesirable to limit university enrollment to students with certain special aptitudes and specialized school training. The teaching profession in this country has been for some years engaged in an attempt to reconcile what is left of the old preparatory school tradition with the demands of the present American ideal of education for all youth.

If I am right in my interpretation of the past, the fluidity of American society and the democratic ideals of the nation were primarily responsible for shaping educational policy in the United States. I believe that a careful student of this country 125 years ago could have come very close to predicting what our present schools and colleges would be like. Indeed, it seems to me, much of what de Tocqueville admired and much of what he questioned in the United States of his day, when translated into terms of schools and universities, is what we find typically American at this moment. The burgeoning pioneer republic, assimilating a variety of national cultures, and combining the industrial revolution with an expanding agriculture, was bound to produce some strange cultural institutions—that is to say, strange as seen through European eyes. But these institutions were not only a product of the new forces but themselves powerful factors in directing the course of our internal history. The men and women trained in the new types of schools, colleges, and universities in the first three decades of this century are the men and women who largely determine the present cultural pattern of the United States.

Some of us can well remember how in the early 1930's our left-wing academic friends in England and on the Continent ridiculed the American ideals of equality of opportunity and equality of respect and our belief in the importance of free competition. Outdated pioneer notions, we were told, not germane to the highly industrialized and class-conscious society of the twentieth century. The road to the future, we were assured by the European radicals of that day, was a socialistic one. It has turned out quite otherwise. Here in America in the last twenty-five years we have evolved a type of economic and social system that was predicted by few European observers. Paul Hoffman has called it "mutual capitalism." Clarence Randall has written about it as follows:

"The United States is a miracle among nations . . . we are still sound financially and all about us we see abundant evidence of constantly rising standards of living. We surge ahead with a vitality and confidence in the future that amaze the world. We do this because we release the unbounded potential for effort of each individual citizen, by rewarding him in accordance with his effort, and by stimulating his imagination through the widest possible freedom of choices in his life . . . We accumulate our resources by rewarding those who produce and save; we restrain selfishness by competition.

"It is no coincidence," he continues, "that our economic way of life and our high standard of living are found together." To which I venture to add that it is no coincidence that our economic way of life and our unique American tradition of education are found together. The internal development of this nation politically, socially, and economically has been bound up with the unfolding of a characteristic American point of view about schools, colleges, and universities.

A century ago American education started to adapt

35

itself to a set of new conditions and succeeded. Today, we face a totally different task. Within a decade this nation has been thrust into a position of enormous responsibility in a highly uncomfortable new world. A century ago the ideas of schools and universities imported from Europe had to be drastically modified to suit the needs of a new type of nation based on new geographic facts and motivated by new ideals. Does the American tradition in education, now approaching the respectable age of one hundred years, likewise stand in need of modification to meet the challenge of our new world, the constricted globe of the mid-twentieth century? My answer would be an emphatic yes. For it seems clear to me that the world conditions we Americans face today are as different from those of ten or twenty years ago as were the conditions faced by our grandparents compared with those of Europe. The contrast now is not between a new nation in process of expanding and older static nations. The contrast now is between the isolated United States of a relatively few years ago, able to struggle through its own social, political, and economic problems largely independent of Europe or of Asia, and a United States one of the two great powers in a world where long distances have disappeared.

Those who remember the "Gay Twenties" would probably agree that the contrast between the third and the sixth decades of this century is for Americans a contrast not of degree but of kind. Whether we like it or not (and there are few in my age group who fail to dislike it at least some of the time) we are living cheek by jowl with some new neighbors, some friendly and helpful, others not. Thanks to the modern airplane, we find ourselves now in much the same situation that Europeans have known for centuries.

It would have been difficult enough for us Americans to accustom ourselves to a globe on which the Atlantic and Pacific Oceans were the equivalent of narrow channels, and the polar regions no longer unexplored and inaccessible. But we must adjust ourselves to a new geography in a period characterized by two phrases, the one hardly less ominous than the other—"a divided world" and "an era of nuclear weapons."

I have no intention of exploring here the implications for the United States that lie hidden in the words "a divided world," but I do want to stress the significance for American education of the altered geography of this age. If, by some miracle, nuclear weapons could be brought under international control and thus eliminated from our thoughts, man's ability to travel through the air at the rate of hundreds of miles an hour would remain unchanged. If the Soviet power should crumble and the Communist bloc disintegrate tomorrow, the American people would still be living under conditions so different from those of a few decades ago as to warrant the use of the phrase "new world." It is, first of all, these conditions that must call forth an imaginative response on the part of our teachers and educational leaders. That this will come, I feel confident. Just as the new conditions in the mid-nineteenth century resulted in the founding of agricultural and mechanical arts colleges and the passage of the land-grant act (Morrill Act) of 1862, so, too, the new conditions of the twentieth century will bring about another American educational transformation.

As long as the world remains divided, we have a very special and heavy responsibility. We are the acknowledged leader of the free nations. Because of our size and our wealth we are the prime defender of all that is involved in the opposition of these free nations to the Soviet ideology. Our schools, colleges, and universities are conscious of the implication for education of this responsibility. The nature of the opposition between the doctrines we hold dear and those of the totalitarian Communist regime must be made clear; this is being done as part of the work of educating our future citizens for life in the American democracy. This job, I have reason to believe, is already well in hand. I have no doubt this phase of American education will continue. But I am not so sure that in certain other respects American education has started even to outline the problems which the new geography has forced upon it.

We have acquired for the first time many near neighbors. A hard-headed appraisal of these neighbors is obviously of first importance. To lay the groundwork for such an appraisal is one of the new tasks of American education. I am well aware of the fact that for many years some educators have urged that our schools and colleges be more concerned with international affairs. But to be quite frank, much of what was written on this subject before the end of World War II is worse than obsolete. The hard realities of the situation in which we now live were not foreseen by those who were active in these affairs ten years or more ago.

First, let us consider the impact of the new tasks on general education. Our future citizens must know what it means to know thoroughly a friendly or a hostile neighbor. We must develop a higher degree of sophistication about foreign affairs, avoiding optimistic sentimentality on the one hand and hopeless cynicism on the other. We need large numbers of men and women who, without themselves being prepared to appraise a foreign nation, realize some of the complexities and difficulties of the task. In this field as in so many others today, it is easy to form a superficial judgment, difficult to grasp what are the essential facts that the experts themselves must come to grips with.

Just as we need an understanding of the way science has developed in order to evaluate the statements of scientific experts, so I think the proverbial man in the street needs an understanding of the way national interests in the past have developed and interlocked. Specifically, this means a far greater emphasis on the study of history. I have long advocated that special attention should be paid in schools and colleges to American history. In the past, I have thought of this largely as internal political and social history. It now seems clear that foreign policy requires at least as much study. And a consideration of the foreign policy of the United States, of course, takes one automatically into the foreign policy of other nations.

More important than the changes in general education will be, I am sure, the changes in specialized education. One obvious example: We need for the first time in our history a very large number of highly competent men and women with talents and tastes for work with people of foreign lands. We shall need to discover such people at an earlier age and provide the educational opportunities for their development. This in part is a question of acquiring skills—the command of foreign tongues—but also of the development of an interest in other lands and peoples. All of which means a vast amount of hard work, long hours of study, patient labor with the printed as well as the spoken word.

In this connection, another look at Europe may not be out of order. Geography to no small degree has moulded the European concept of what is required of the schools in the way of teaching skills. Holland and Switzerland illustrate the point I have in mind. In those countries no one is considered educated who cannot speak fluently at least two foreign languages (and I emphasize the phrase at least). The revolution in transportation has made the capitals of France, Germany, Italy, and Spain almost as close to Washington as those capitals were to each other at the time of World War I. I need labor the point no further. That the place of foreign language instruction, like the place of history, in the future curricula of American schools will be very different from the past is an obvious prediction. That this change will make schooldays easier not even the most enthusiastic linguist is likely to maintain. The new position of the United States of a shrunken globe places new burdens on all of us, including all our youth.

The demands of military service in themselves are having, and will continue to have, a great effect on our educational institutions. But quite apart from these considerations which apply to our able-bodied young

41

men, the burden is on all our young people, men and women alike. Their potential capacities are this nation's greatest asset. The time of youth is the time for developing these capacities; to the extent this time is wasted, America of the future will be poorer, less able to shoulder the heavy loads the new world conditions place upon us. And even the most enthusiastic supporter of American education must admit that a great deal of time is wasted in school and college.

In 1950 the Educational Policies Commission of the National Educational Association published a pamphlet entitled *Education of the Gifted*. In the foreword it was stated, "Acquaintance with present educational practices has convinced the Commission that the gifted members of the total school population constitute a minority which is too largely neglected." It would be out of place for me to detail the recommendations of this report, though I am tempted to do so, as I was one of its authors. But I can sum up what we had in mind by quoting the following sentence: "To capitalize the rich resources of human talent which gifted children and youth possess, the schools and colleges must give special attention to the education of their gifted students."

This call to the schools and colleges was written before it was as clear as now what the nature of the postwar period would be. The last five years have spelled out for us the consequences of living in a constricted yet divided world. These consequences surely underline the need for educational reforms in regard to gifted children. For in this difficult period, if the United States is to fulfill its role, it will need to utilize to the fullest possible extent "the rich resources of human talent" in each generation.

Let me give two examples: There has been an increasing concern in recent years with our failure to educate a sufficient number of scientists and engineers. That is to say, a number sufficient to man adequately our industries and our national defense establishments. The colleges blame the schools for inadequate preparation (particularly in mathematics), and the schools blame the taxpayers for not providing sufficient funds to pay for first-rate teachers of science and mathematics. Both criticisms are correct to my way of thinking; as to the second, I shall have more to say in the concluding pages of this book. As to the first, the difficulty is in no small part due to our failure to identify at a relatively young age those boys and girls who have more than the average talent for mathematics. If such pupils were identified (and tests for this purpose seem to be at hand) and then were stimulated to proceed relatively rapidly with their studies, a respectable fraction of the incoming freshmen of the better colleges would have sufficient mathematical

43

aptitude to tackle the physics and chemistry courses with both enthusiasm and success. At present, a number of college students who formerly had the ambition of becoming scientists drop out once they run into the difficulties of freshman physics, chemistry, and mathematics.

Similar considerations apply to the study of foreign languages. As in the case of mathematics, I doubt the wisdom of attempting to force any large proportion of our high school students into the type of "stiff" courses of instruction characteristic of the European university-preparatory schools. It is true that lack of native ability may to a considerable degree be compensated for by diligent study. But the social pressures which in Europe have forced the students headed for a university to work extremely hard at school (by American standards) do not exist in the United States and are not likely to exist in the near future. Too many American families (even in the higher income brackets) ask the headmaster (even of a private school), Why should Johnny have to continue with mathematics, which is so hard for him? After all, we don't want him to be an Einstein! And as for foreign languages, why should our son keep on with his French, when, as far as anyone can tell, he may never need it? The parental demand for a "thorough" European type of education hardly exists in the United States even among the 5 or 10 per cent of the population whose sons in older countries would be forced "willy-nilly" to study what they were told to and not necessarily what they liked. And in the American public high school as well as in the private college-preparatory school, the attitude of the student is not conducive to taking on hard tasks of "book learning" because someone in authority says it is important. American sons and daughters, unlike their European counterparts, have learned at a young age to ask and demand a rational answer to the question "Why should I do that?"

The way out of this educational quandary lies in identifying scholastic talent young (in mathematics or foreign langauges or both) and then providing for teachers who will stimulate the selected students to do their utmost because they want to and as a matter of pride. The colleges must do their part by accepting the selected students on such a basis that their unusual high school accomplishments will be recognized and suitably rewarded. The spirit of competition is not, to my mind, something to be deplored. If kept in bounds by a spirit of "fair play," it is a healthy aspect of our tremendous emphasis on sports. There is no reason why the same type of motivation could not be utilized in the study of mathematics and foreign languages, provided, as in athletics, selection of the naturally talented is accepted as a matter of course; and provided that public

45

opinion becomes convinced of the importance of the undertaking.

No one expects a majority of school children to learn to play a musical instrument, but nearly everyone would like to have the musically gifted encouraged to develop their talents. Our attitude toward music might well serve as a pattern as to the attitude which we Americans should take in regard to the education of our youth whose native ability lies in the fields of words or numbers. Local enthusiasm needs to be aroused for discovering and adequately educating those who are intellectually gifted. On a national scale the recently established Merit Scholarship Corporation is an important step in this direction. Identification of talent, motivation through aroused interest and competition should enable our schools to utilize much more than now the rich sources of talent in each generation.

What I have just suggested and the changes I shall later propose for our colleges and universities can be accomplished by modifications in our educational practices so slight that they will not jeopardize the essence of the American tradition in education. We need not retreat one step from our own goal of providing education for all (and I mean all) American youth. For, let me make it plain, I am neither prophesying nor recommending abandonment of those basic principles that characterize our schools and colleges as contrasted with the European. Equality of opportunity for all children and equality of respect among all occupational groups are two doctrines that are as significant for our future as for our past. These are the fundamental premises of American education. Every citizen needs to understand them; every citizen needs to realize how they differ from the premises in other lands. He will then be more ready to support in every possible way the further development of the American tradition of education and to adapt it to the new world. If one understands why American schools have developed as they have, one will be the more ready to support those schools in such a way as to make them correspond to the needs of the new world in which we live.

3. SOME BASIC PROBLEMS OF

AMERICAN EDUCATION

IN THE preceding essays I have treated the two main functions of a university, teaching and research, as though they were totally unrelated. I have written of the work of scholars and scientists as though those engaged in the search for "warranted beliefs" had no concern with the instruction of young men and women. I have contrasted the European and American systems of education without reference to the significance of the universities as centers of research and scholarship. Furthermore, by focusing attention on the long-range aspects of scholarly undertakings, I have omitted any consideration of the role of universities in promoting the applications of science to medicine, to industry, to agriculture, and to national defense.

The artificial isolation of two components of a complex situation simplifies the presentation of the characteristic features. But merely juxtaposing the components fails to give an adequate picture of the whole. Only by considering the interrelation of the several functions of a university can one attempt to formulate answers to such practical questions as the following: What should be the relation of research to teaching in an undergraduate college? In a professional faculty? How should research be financed? What are the priorities in terms of the expenditure of public moneys? Is education for *all* American youth more important than the professional education of a selected few, and are both more important than research? (In view of the vast expansion in our educational facilities required by the wave of increased population, these last two questions, difficult as they are to formulate or answer, are basic to much of the current discussion of the way our educational institutions should expand.)

The pages that follow represent an effort to bring together the two themes of the preceding essays in terms applicable to the situation that now confronts American educators, or rather I should say confronts all American citizens. For the tremendous increase in the number of school children caused by the drastic upswing in the birthrate during World War II has already presented the taxpayer with a sizable financial problem. In a few years, to the costs of expanding our schools will be added very large costs for the expansion of either our colleges or universities or both. This unexpected complication of the educational scene (unexpected twenty years ago) makes it doubly necessary for the layman to interest himself in certain educational problems which were already under discussion before the impact of World War II upset the functioning of our colleges.

Public demand has shaped the evolution of American education, and informed public opinion will largely determine the future pattern. Therefore, in this period of unexpected forced expansion it seems important for leaders of opinion to be familiar with the various alternatives that seem possible in regard to the arrangements of our schools and colleges. For this reason I have attempted to analyze for the general reader such practical problems as the financing of research in pure and applied science, the length and cost of professional training, and the type of education beyond the high school to be provided for those who do not intend to enter a profession. Of course, the details of the organization and management of schools, colleges, and universities must be left to school boards, boards of trustees, faculties, and administrative officers. But some knowledge of our present practices and the possibilities for development is essential for a public discussion of what course American education should take in the next two decades. Therefore I offer no apologies for a consideration in these concluding pages of mundane matters and an exclusive concern with the educational problems of one nation—the United States.

To introduce a matter-of-fact, down-to-earth note at the outset, let me remind the reader that research and education are highly expensive undertakings. But let me add a warning to the effect that the methods of public accounting for the expenditures are very often such as to obscure the answer to the question who pays the bills. For example, while it is correct to state that adequate provision for professional education and research in the United States today requires both private and public support on a large scale, it would be false to say that no research institutes and no educational institutions could be self-supporting (that is, operate without annual gifts, endowment, or government support). Private industrial research organizations operating on a consulting basis do make money; more than one professional school within a university has had in the recent past a considerable excess of receipts from tuition over expenditures. It is worth examining those exceptions to the general rule in order to bring to light certain basic factors in regard to both advanced education and research.

The case of the private consulting firm of research chemists and engineers might seem to be beside the point, if it were not for the fact that in the last fifteen years the amount of applied research carried out in our universities has increased enormously. Now applied research in physics, chemistry, and engineering usually brings immediate benefits to some industrial firm (or firms) or to some branch of the United States Government (in the last ten years principally the Department of Defense). The question has been raised more than once why should those who thus directly benefit not pay for what they get? Why should not research in applied fields including work done for the Government be placed on a strictly business basis? It has even been suggested that in the case of industrial research and discoveries that can be patented the institutions in question make a profit sufficient to support their entire scientific research program. Somewhat similar questions were raised in faculties of engineering and applied science long before World War II. But it was the tremendous expansion of research budgets immediately after the war and the difficulties of financing universities that led to a widespread discussion of the issues. What was once only a problem for a few professors of engineering who had a profitable consulting practice on the side or who held profitable patents has now become a matter of interest to all faculties.

In at least one university a start has been made in the direction of abolishing the traditional practice according to which a professor is free to take on whatever consulting work he likes and for whatever fee.

In the past the only limitation on the liberty of the professor has been that his outside activities must not interfere with his teaching and not be contrary to the public interest. Such an arrangement which I believe still continues in almost all the leading universities of the free world allows, of course, some professors with a profitable consulting practice to earn a much higher income than their colleagues whose expert knowledge is not in great demand. The proponents of a drastic change in the long-established tradition argue not only that such inequalities in income are inimical to the spirit of true scholarship but that the possibilities of personal profit from professional work tempt a professor to turn his attention to immediate problems instead of advancing his field of science by investigations of fundamental matters. To which the answer is often given that the remedy suggested is far worse than the disease.

Under the proposed new procedure either professors would cease to do consulting work and thereby cut themselves off from practical affairs or the university would become a consulting firm and the professors employees. In the latter case the pressures will be for *more* applied research, more outside activities, and the long-range scholarly activities will suffer. There are practical administrative problems in addition. Are textbooks, popular professional books, and lectures to

54

be placed in the same category as consulting work? How about a professor of literature who may write a highly successful novel? But these are relatively trivial objections. The issues that are worth examining cluster around the central fact that an academic scientist today (including a social scientist) like the engineer of fifty years ago can often devote a certain amount of his time and energy to immediate problems and he (or his university) be well paid for the effort. But so too can the professor of medicine or surgery. Indeed, the history of the medical schools in the United States is bound up with basically the same questions as those raised by the proposal to have all the income a professor earns by outside activities accrue to the university. It is therefore relevant to consider briefly what has happened to medical education in the United States in the last fifty years.

At the turn of the century, medical education in the United States was financed in the last analysis primarily by the profitable practice of a few eminent physicians and surgeons; so, too, were clinical investigations (research in such basic medical sciences as biochemistry and physiology had hardly started). These may seem incredible statements to those not familiar with the story but they are no exaggeration. Before the Flexner report, the chairs of medicine and surgery were occupied by doctors and surgeons engaged in highly successful practice; their work as professors was on the side. The establishment of full-time professorships a generation ago brought about a major revolution not only in medical education but in clinical research. This was only possible because large sums were made available for endowment for privately supported universities and by increased appropriations from state legislatures. For in place of paying a professor an almost trivial sum, most medical schools established a salary scale for full-time professors that was somewhere near what a successful doctor or surgeon might expect to earn from his private practice. By thus focusing the attention of the professors of medicine and surgery on the academic side of their work, clinical investigation became a main concern. This it never could be as long as the professors in question were deeply involved in a lucrative private practice. The great success of this revolutionary change in the medical schools would seem to provide a powerful argument for putting professors of all the faculties on the same footing, namely for abolishing all *private* practice as consultants. But a close examination of the situation reveals flaws in the supposed analogy.

In the first place, doctors and surgeons can forward their profession only by being in contact with patients. The hospital is the center of clinical research in its most theoretical aspects as well as the place where private patients are visited. The dichotomy between the study of fundamental problems and applied consulting work characteristic of chemistry or physics is replaced by another conflict of interests. The doctor or surgeon must choose between attention to cases which throw light on a particular medical or surgical problem and attention to patients irrespective of their ills who can afford to pay handsome fees. It was to enable the professor to pick his patients primarily in terms of his research interest that full-time medical and surgical chairs were established. In the second place, experience has shown that where the full-time principle has been consistently employed, an over-developed interest in the fees from patients can readily re-enter the picture and in a way highly unfavorable to research. It is easy, for example, for the budgetary pressures to become so great that the head of a department established for the study of some specialty will scan with anxious eyes the receipts from the patients' fees that are credited to his department. When this happens he and his staff are under strong temptation to act as did the part-time professors of previous time; fees rather than research have the first priority. That something akin to this would happen in many departments of several faculties seems almost inevitable

57

if the general principle should be established that income from the consulting activities of a professor should come to the university.

A modification of the full-time scheme in medicine which is more in line with the traditional practice in other faculties has much to recommend it. It has been successfully in operation in one leading medical school for many years. Under this arrangement, a full-time professor is bound by an unwritten gentleman's agreement to engage in not more than a limited private practice the income from which shall not exceed his salary; the fees are received by the professor, not the school or hospital. Like the full-time professors in the schools where no private patients may be seen, these professors are fully committed to clinical investigations and teaching; they are in no sense part-time teachers. To be sure they are free to supplement their salaries within the limits described, but each professor's conscience determines how much time and energy he may devote to the income-producing practice without detriment to his work as a teacher and clinical investigator.

Such a modified full-time basis with no fees accruing to the institution seems to me ideal for medical schools; it also sets a pattern suitable for all faculties. But it means, of course, that the professors must be paid adequate salaries. This in turn requires a large annual budget, the income side of which must be supplied by income from endowment, annual gifts, taxpayers' money, or tuition fees. In the case of first-rate medical schools receipts from tuition are always relatively minor because of the small size of the classes. Therefore, medical education and medical research must be heavily subsidized by private philanthropy or the state. The diminution of the effective purchasing power of the income from endowment that occurred in the 1940's has been a major disaster for medical education. As has been made evident by the National Fund for Medical Education in the appeal to industry for funds, we have already lost many of the gains of the revolution of a generation ago; faced with extreme budgetary difficulties, medical schools are more and more reverting to the use of part-time teachers. The consequences of such steps backward are not evident at once; but unless the budgets of the faculties of medicine can be adequately supported over the coming years, both as professional training institutions and as research centers, our medical schools will suffer a deterioration which will be catastrophic.

A physician or surgeon heavily engaged in his own private practice may be an excellent teacher in a medical school insofar as time allows; many such teachers today supplement the instruction of full-time professors. But a medical faculty comprised only of such professional men would be a very different place from what the leading schools are today. This is above all true as regards research, the relation of research to teaching and the training of future clinical investigators. The progress of medical science has already been slowed down; if the arrangements of fifty years ago are once again brought back medical schools will no longer be centers of research. Here we are dealing with progress in an applied science. An even more drastic change in our universities would occur if we imagine that all the departments of physics and chemistry were staffed with physicists, engineers, and chemists from nearby industrial firms who would devote say six hours a week to giving the necessary lectures (and this is all the actual time that professors in the physical sciences often spend in a classroom). The content of the lectures might be excellent, the practical note introduced might be highly beneficial, even the laboratory instruction might be adequately organized with young assistants; but there would be no scientific faculty in the university. There would be no investigative work going on within the university laboratory; the interest of the part-time professors under the conditions imagined would be quite properly focused on their industrial work. There would be little interest in and no study of basic problems unless the industrial firms chose to support such work in their own laboratories.

The grim hypothetical picture I have just painted

of science faculties manned solely by part-time industrial scientists is, alas, not so far distant from reality as some lay readers might imagine. There is only a slight difference between my hypothetical industrial chemist devoting six hours a week to lecturing in a university and a university professor spending all *but* six hours engaged on outside consulting work. And unless the university pays an adequate salary, the temptation for a professor to turn himself into a consultant is very great. Furthermore, unless the university provides first-rate facilities for research on basic problems and in its *policy of promotion recognizes the paramount importance of research,* the natural outlet for the creative activity of the scientist may be consulting work. We are clearly dealing here with subtle intangible human factors and therefore not with a black or white proposition. If American universities are to be productive centers of research, we must on the one hand leave the professor free, on the other arrange for him conditions that favor his devoting essentially all his time to those problems of research which seem to him most rewarding—not in terms of dollars but in terms of the advance of his own science.

Steps to put a university on a self-supporting basis as a research institution are extremely dangerous even as regards the welfare of an applied science like medicine. Staffing a university with part-time teachers, or driving professors to become in fact part-time teachers, endangers the institution as a center of research and as a training ground for further investigators. Furthermore, all moves which tend to force the attention of professors to immediate problems reinforce the factors inherent in our age which are inimical to the health of the university tradition. There may have been times when faculties needed to be stimulated to concern themselves with the world around them; there may be nations, today, where the universities are too much ivory towers. But in this period of technology and in the United States, all the forces are working in the opposite direction. If the long-range values of the creative work of scholars are not to be buried under an avalanche of studies of immediate pressing matters, every effort must be made to develop at least a certain number of American universities as centers for the study of basic problems, as homes of scholarship and learning. And to this end the financing of these institutions and the income of the professors must be independent of the practical outcome of the scientific investigations.

The phrase "at least a certain number of American universities" was used advisedly in the preceding paragraph. It is time we were more frank in our discussion of American education as to the enormous differences between institutions that are called universities.

The significant lines of demarcation are not in terms of size (some of the best are the smallest, some of the largest are the least scholarly) nor in terms of private versus state-supported. Among the dozen leading universities I should place at least three or four state universities, while a number of universities that hardly warrant the label are private, nonsectarian institutions. Such institutions often perform a valuable service to the communities in which they are located and may be outstanding in the training of personnel for the so-called semiprofessions, but they are in no sense centers of research or scholarship. In some of them research and teaching are in fact completely separated because research activities among the professors are conspicuous by their absence! But this may also be true, from time to time, of course, of a few faculties within a university which is pre-eminent for its position as a scholarly center in many fields.

It is among such faculties composed only of teachers with no scholarly interest that one finds examples of the situation already mentioned, namely, a teaching entity whose receipts from tuition are larger than the expenditures. The existence of such units within a university is rarely advertised and the excess of income is usually absorbed in financing some other faculty or department. But it is worth noting that in certain vocational fields it has been possible to organize insti-

63

tutions in such a way that the student more than pays the actual costs. Large classes, overworked and poorly paid teachers are the standard formula for attaining such results; the use of part-time teachers often enables the faculty in question to have on its rolls some competent people but, as in the case of part-time professors of medicine, their commitment is not to their academic work. These exceptional instances of self-supporting teaching units are worth noting because their existence underlines a fact which few laymen appreciate, namely, that the cost of advanced education depends on the type and quality of education that is offered. It is possible to train (but not educate) technicians in certain fields at a relatively low cost; this cost may be covered by what students are ready to pay for or by a relatively small appropriation from the state legislatures. But such types of training do not produce educated men or women; they represent the extreme case of the separation of the teaching function from the traditions of a university.

The cases where instruction of university students is supported by tuition fees are relatively rare, but that a great deal of such instruction is carried on by inadequately paid teachers is a fact. In such cases neither the salaries paid nor the scholarly facilities (laboratories and libraries) attract even second-class talent to the staff. But even some universities that are able to attract and keep a competent group of teachers are unable to support scholarly investigations; here the professors' load of teaching is too heavy, there are no funds for books, travel, or laboratory equipment; promotion is based solely on teaching ability as demonstrated in handling large groups of students. Probably it would be safe to say that a majority of American students who receive a bachelor's degree study in an institution where little or no first-rate research or scholarly work is in progress. Such being the case someone may well ask, why not make a clean sweep of it and have one set of institutions concerned only with research, the others only with teaching?

A few who have looked with despair through Europeanized eyes on the chaos of the American educational scene seem to have come to some such conclusion. Research institutes have been established in this century not only for specialized sciences but for scholarship in general. To my mind this has not been a step in the right direction; further such developments would have extremely unfortunate consequences for the United States. Why? Because the education and training of professional men and women I am convinced can only be satisfactorily accomplished where research and teaching are effectively combined.

As to the necessity of having research in progress where scientists are being trained, there would seem to be little room for argument. Obviously future investigators can only be developed by being immersed in research. But the word research covers a wide field of activities today and it is possible to have a scientific faculty primarily concerned with applied science where only immediate practical problems are under investigation. To be sure, as far as methods are concerned there is little difference between pure and applied science, as the Marxist writers on science are fond of reminding us. But that little difference makes an enormous difference in the spirit of the institution. Roughly speaking, where fundamental scientific problems are under investigation, the theoretical component of the scientific framework is in evidence as compared to the empirical. A recognition of this fact has led engineering schools in the United States within a generation to stress the importance of basic research in the physical sciences. Viewing the matter solely in terms of training scientists and engineers, therefore, I believe it is not too much to say that to the extent that fundamental research is in progress in institutes divorced from teaching, the development of talent is impeded.

The training of scientists is of such obvious importance to the national welfare that I have no doubt many educational institutions will continue to flourish where scientific research provides the background for technological training. But the nature of the general education to be provided for those scientists and for other professional men (lawyers and doctors, for example) is another story. It is at this point that the differences between the universities on the two sides of the Iron Curtain become evident. As I indicated in the opening pages of this book, as far as the training of scientists and engineers is concerned, the countries under Communist control differ little from the nations of the free world. But the nature of the general education is as different as white is from black. We in the free world through our schools, colleges, and universities seek to perpetuate that tradition of Western culture which emphasizes diversity, controversy, and tolerance. The Soviets seek uniformity and strict adherence to the dogmas of the creed of Marxism-Leninism.

Now it would be my contention that the education of professional men and women should be carried out in institutions where free inquiry is rampant. For if the free world is to preserve that spirit which has made possible the growth of Western culture, the future leaders must as young men be impregnated with this spirit. The students of the professions should early come to know the significance of dissent. They should be exposed to an intellectual atmosphere where vital differences of opinion are not merely tolerated but

67

encouraged, where at least one battle royal of ideas has captured the attention of the community of scholars. This is easier to accomplish in some fields of learning than in others—in science and medicine more difficult than in law, in law more difficult than in philosophy or economics. As I indicated earlier, the role of heresy in science is only appreciated by examining the total development of scientific thought over many, many decades. The current controversies are of too short duration nowadays to be impressive examples of a struggle of beliefs. To offset this inherent lack in the education and training of the scientific professions, a study of the history of science is strongly to be recommended. But more important is the existence in each institution where professional leaders are being trained of strong departments dealing with subjects which by their nature are highly controversial. And by strong departments I mean departments composed of able and aggressive scholars deeply concerned with both teaching and the advance of learning. The presence of such professors affects the spirit of the entire institution; without scholarly controversy a university ceases to be a suitable place for education for the professions, however satisfactory may be the training offered. This is the reason why one must regret the absence from a university of every scholar and investigator who is at work in a separate institution. At best there are not enough able scholars to meet the needs of all our universities, and every individual who is separated from a community of students and teachers is a heavy loss to our educational forces.

Perhaps some readers will be willing to grant my thesis as an ideal but be ready then to show the impossibility of its realization in America today, particularly in view of the impending increase in the number of college students. If so, I am prepared to argue not only for the ideal but for the possibility of coming nearer to its realization in the next few decades *just because of the growth of the population.* To muster my arguments, I must first, however, ask the reader to turn his attention to those characteristics of the total American educational scene which differentiate it from the European. At present, something like a third of the American youth who are of an age to enter college at least start some sort of full-time education beyond the high school. Approximately half this number, or 10 to 15 per cent of the age group, complete a four-year course; of these, in turn, less than a quarter obtain a second degree by studying in some professional school in a university. The statistics are complicated by the fact that engineering professional education is usually finished in four years and by the fact that a certain number of doctors and lawyers do not complete college before embarking on their professional studies. But one may estimate with some assurance that not more than three or four out of every hundred boys of high school age end up with a professional degree from an accredited institution. This is not an appreciably higher percentage, by the way, than on the European continent or in Great Britain.

The unique features of the American pattern are not to be found by examining our professional education. They are found by noting first that there is no separation of pre-college or pre-university students at an early age (except for a very few who attend private boarding schools or country day schools), and second, that a large fraction of the youth eighteen to twenty years of age is enrolled in some college or university. That both characteristics are firmly embedded in the American tradition, I have no doubt. They will not be altered in the future; talk about limiting college enrollment to a relatively small elite is quite beside the point. A larger rather than a smaller fraction of the youth will in the future enroll in post-high school institutions. *But it by no means follows that almost all these students should be accommodated in four-year colleges or universities.* There would be no inconsistency with our educational ideals if local two-year colleges were to enroll as many as a half of the boys and girls who wished to engage in formal studies beyond the high school. At present the number of two-year colleges is relatively few and their total enrollment small. But if they were vigorously supported and expanded as the wave of increased numbers hit the universities, the distribution of youth among the various types of educational institutions might be radically altered without diminution of the percentage of youths receiving an advanced education. If this were done, the composition of the student bodies in the universities would change without any reduction in size; the emphasis would shift toward professional education. That such a shift would be beneficial for those universities now aiming at becoming first-rate scholarly institutions few would question. On the other hand, if some such development does not occur, the pressure of applicants on the tax-supported universities will force a rapid and enormous increase in the teaching staff. The quality of the faculty is bound to deteriorate and more than one promising center of research and professional education will become a training institution.

There would seem to be great advantages, therefore, in preparing now for the time, only a few years hence, when the flood of college students will be at hand. And those preparations, to my mind, should consist primarily in the establishment of many local two-year colleges. They should be planned to attract the large majority of the youths who now enter a four-year

71

college or university with little intention of completing a four-year course of study. The fact is often overlooked that about one-half of the students who enter our colleges and universities drop out during the first two years.

As the size of the graduating classes of the high schools increases, more and more graduates should be induced to stay at home and attend the local college. I use the word induce because in order to accomplish the change here advocated it will be necessary to develop strong attractive forces in the two-year colleges. It will be necessary also for our universities to be content with keeping their present size and aim not at a larger student body but at a somewhat different distribution of aptitudes and interests in the freshman class. For all this to be accomplished, the American public must be convinced that the proposed changes are in the best interest of the nation. This, I believe, can be demonstrated to the citizens primarily interested in the education of those young people who are *not* going to become professional men or women (some 95 per cent of our youth). It can also be demonstrated to those who are primarily concerned with the relatively few who will enter the professions. And finally, it can be demonstrated to those who wish this nation to play an important role in scientific research and the advancement of learning.

Basic Problems of American Education

For those who regard universities as first of all institutions for research, scholarly work, and professional education, the advantages in changing the composition of the entering classes are obvious. So, too, are the advantages of eliminating the large number who now drop out after one or two years of study. The dangers of swamping our universities with a sudden influx of numbers are equally apparent. There is no need to argue for a course of action that would make the publicly supported universities more scholarly and more professional without any decrease in their present size. That is to say, there is no need to argue the case to those who understand the significance of having the leaders of the free world educated professionally on campuses where the scholarly spirit of free inquiry is dominant.

For those whose interests are focused on the education of all our future citizens, irrespective of their vocations, the proposal to channel a large proportion of high school graduates into local colleges instead of publicly supported universities also has much to recommend it. First, because a local two-year college can often take care of a boy or girl looking for a short general education better than can a university. The combination of vocational training and general studies offered may yield results more lasting than exposure to instruction in enormous classes in a university.

Psychologically, there are often great advantages in being in a smaller and more familiar group. Second, because there is a certain relation between the expansion of our state universities and the type of education offered to *all* the youth of the state in the high schools. The taxpayers' money supports public education at all levels. At a time of forced expansion, as at present, there is under the best of circumstances not enough money to do what should be done to handle the problem of increased numbers in the high schools. With the exception of a few fortunate localities, teachers' salaries are far too low. The effects of this inadequate salary scale are to be seen particularly in the high schools and in the failure to recruit enough first-rate teachers of science and mathematics. Now the more expensive it is to finance the publicly supported colleges, the less likely it is that the high schools will be adequately financed. And it is clear that local two-year colleges are a far less expensive form of advanced education than that provided by a university, unless the university is doing a wretched job for its freshman and sophomore classes.

The educational as well as the economic and sociological advantages of an expansion of our two-year colleges have been set forth by a number of authors (including the present writer) in the last few years. I do not propose to repeat these arguments in this book. I would like to repeat, however, a recommendation that may be regarded as heretical but in the light of a realistic analysis of American colleges is not so heretical as its sounds. This is that two-year colleges regularly accord a bachelor's degree (with some appropriate designation) to their graduates. I am well aware of the distress that such a proposal arouses in four-year colleges and universities. "Lowering of standards" is the cry. But if any objective study were ever made of the standards now prevailing for the awarding of a bachelor's degree by four-year institutions, it would be evident that no standards (other than tuition paid and years of exposure) are in fact in existence. We have long since, in the United States, abandoned the ideal which still holds in other nations, that a degree is equally valid no matter what institution may award it. Such being the case, the completion of a good two-year course would more than equal in educational value the finishing of four-year courses of study in certain institutions.

Those who are versed in academic arithmetic and the ways of advanced education may be ready to point out that I have only contrasted two-year local colleges with universities. I have hardly referred to the four-year liberal arts college which has no university affiliation. This is true, and the reason is that very few of these are publicly supported. Therefore, the question of their expansion does not affect the taxpayer directly. Furthermore, there is such a variety of four-year colleges with such varying types of faculties and standards that generalizations in this field are sure to be misunderstood. At one end of the spectrum stand those colleges whose endowment has been sufficient to enable them to recruit a first-rate faculty. As several New England colleges have so well proved in the last quarter of a century, such faculties may provide an excellent education for future professional men. While these colleges can hardly be centers of research in the sciences (the laboratory facilities are too expensive, graduate students are not at hand), the quality of the scholarship of the faculty may be excellent in history, government, economics, literature, and philosophy. And it is these controversial subjects that are of so great importance in determining the intellectual atmosphere.

At the other end of the spectrum of the four-year liberal arts colleges are institutes which are hardly more than vocational training centers. They may, as I indicated earlier, be almost self-supporting because of the tuition fees. Some form of business education is usually combined with a formal smattering of the liberal arts. Whether it requires four years for the completion of some of the programs offered has been questioned by competent critics. The temptation is great for an institution that depends largely on tuition fees to prolong its course of study. Between the two extremes lie the more than one thousand colleges that are recorded as offering four-year courses in the United States. The future of each one is of deep concern to its alumni, friends, faculty, and trustees. Each case has to be considered separately in the light of the history of the college and the local situation. Some might decide to become primarily two-year colleges, others to emphasize even more than at present the education of students headed for a university. But important as the future of these private four-year colleges may be, the issue I am presenting does not turn on their expansion or their retaining their present size. It is the future size and goal of our tax-supported universities and the future expansion of our two-year tax-supported colleges that confront the American taxpayer with a basic choice. State by state, the citizens must reappraise the publicly supported educational system from top to bottom and decide what adjustment must be made to handle the vast increase in the numbers of the youth.

But more important still than a decision about two-year colleges is the answer to the fundamental question: Are we ready to support our schools, colleges, and universities so that the promise implicit in our educational ideals may be realized in the coming years?

77

The Citadel of Learning

What is at stake is both the American educational tradition and the welfare of our citadels of learning. The desperate state of the tax-supported schools in many localities is so well known that no words are required here to underline the urgency of their needs. The recruiting and training of the teachers for our elementary and secondary schools require a new and imaginative approach in order to meet the exigencies of the sudden expansion of our schools. But unless the educational budgets can be very much expanded, all efforts to improve the quality of the staffs of our public schools will come to nothing. The level of teachers' salaries must be greatly raised.

Do we as Americans realize how extraordinary an instrument of democracy we have forged in the last hundred years? Are we ready to place high on our list of priorities not only the expansion but the improvement of our public schools? Are we anxious to find ways, even if they are expensive, to do far more than now for the education of the talented? Are we ready to support a considerable number of universities as centers for research and professional education where the spiritual inheritance of the free world may be preserved and fostered? And not only to support them financially but guard them against the traditional enemies of learning: that is to say, mobilize public opinion to beat off attacks by the forces of ignorance, prejudice, and intolerance? These are the basic questions, to my mind, that must be answered by the citizens of this nation. It is not too much to say that the future of the free world for the balance of this century depends to a large extent on the answers given.